Greatest SPEECHES

JONNY ZUCKER

Badger Publishing Limited
Oldmedow Road,
Hardwick Industrial Estate,
King's Lynn PE30 4JJ
Telephone: 01438 791037

www.badgerlearning.co.uk

6 8 10 9 7 5

Greatest Speeches ISBN 978-1-78464-132-0

Text © Jonny Zucker 2015

Complete work © Badger Publishing Limited 2015

All rights reserved. No part of this publication may be reproduced, stored in any form or by any means mechanical, electronic, recording or otherwise without the prior permission of the publisher.

The right of Jonny Zucker to be identified as author of this work has been asserted by him in accordance with the Copyright, Designs and Patents Act 1988.

Publisher: Susan Ross
Senior Editor: Danny Pearson
Publishing Assistant: Claire Morgan
Designer: Cathryn Gilbert
Series Consultant: Dee Reid
Copyeditor: Cheryl Lanyon

Photos: Cover Image:/Stringer/Getty images
Page 5: © Jurgen Ziewe/Alamy
Page 6: Gill Allen/REX
Page 7: © Xinhua/Alamy
Page 8: Courtesy Everett Collection/REX
Page 10: © North Wind Picture Archives/Alamy
Page 12: Courtesy Everett Collection/REX
Page 14: Sipa Press/REX
Page 16: Nara Archives/REX
Page 18: REX
Page 20: Courtesy Everett Collection/REX, Greg Mathieson/REX
Page 22: Action Press/REX
Page 24: Roger-Viollet/REX
Page 26: Action Press/REX
Page 28: © Europa Newswire/Alamy
Page 30: A.M.P.A.S/REX

Attempts to contact all copyright holders have been made.
If any omitted would care to contact Badger Learning, we will be happy to make appropriate arrangements.

Greatest SPEECHES

Contents

1. The power of words — 5
2. War and freedom — 8
3. To change the world — 16
4. The president's speech — 24
5. Famous Faces — 28

Questions — 31

Index — 32

Vocabulary

apartheid
illegal
imprisoned
parliament

persuaded
presidential
promoting
terrorists

1. THE POWER OF WORDS

Speaking up

There is a famous saying: 'Actions speak louder than words', but sometimes words can be really powerful.

There are lots of examples of how a speech has changed people's minds or made them think about things in a new light.

- In 1964, Nelson Mandela was put in prison by the white rulers of South Africa because he said that black people should have the same rights as white people.

  When he was finally released, Mandela went on to give many more speeches about equality.

- In 1940, during World War Two, the people of Britain were thinking that they could never win. Then, Winston Churchill, the Prime Minister, made a famous speech which lifted the nation's hearts.

- Sixteen-year-old Malala Yousafzai was shot and nearly killed by terrorists in Pakistan in 2012. After that, she started speaking up about the rights of children all over the world to be free to learn, and not to live in fear.

A speech can change the course of history.

2. WAR AND FREEDOM

An end to slavery

In 1789, British Member of Parliament, William Wilberforce, made a famous speech about ending the terrible slave trade.

His words did not change the law, but he never gave up, making speech after speech to stop slavery. Finally, in 1807, the Slave Trade Act was passed and it became illegal to buy and sell slaves.

William Wilberforce speaking in the House of Commons said:

> " I determine to forget all my other fears, and I march forward with a firmer step in the full assurance that my cause will bear me out, and that I shall be able to justify upon the clearest principles, every resolution in my hand, the avowed end of which is, the total abolition of the slave trade. "

Wilberforce used his speech to explain that he was not afraid and that he would carry on fighting for his cause. He said he could back-up all his reasons for wanting to end the slave trade.

The women's vote

In 1872, Susan B. Anthony was fined $100 for voting in the American presidential election. Why? Because it was illegal for women to vote. She was so furious with this fine that she started travelling around America speaking up for women's right to vote.

WOW! facts

American women got the vote in 1920. Susan B. Anthony never paid the fine.

In 1873, one of her speeches included these words:

> It was we, the people; not we, the white male citizens... who formed the Union (The United States).
>
> And we formed it, not to give the blessings of liberty, but to secure them; not to the half of ourselves and the half of our posterity, but to the whole people — women as well as men.

Anthony used her speech to argue that all the people, not just the white men, formed the United States and it was formed to give freedom to everyone – including women.

We shall fight on the beaches

In early 1940, thousands of British and Allied troops were trapped on the beach at Dunkirk in France. The Nazis were getting closer and closer. Hundreds of British boats, from warships to tiny fishing boats, crossed the English Channel to bring the 338,000 men back to the UK.

After this amazing rescue, British Prime Minister, Winston Churchill, made this rousing speech to parliament:

> We shall fight on the seas and oceans, we shall fight with growing confidence and growing strength in the air, we shall defend our island whatever the cost may be, we shall fight on the beaches, we shall fight on the landing grounds, we shall fight in the fields and in the streets, we shall fight in the hills; we shall never surrender.

Although Churchill's speeches have become very famous, at the time, some members of parliament criticised them for not being 'moving' enough.

Long walk to freedom

Nelson Mandela was held in prison for 27 years. It would have been easy for him to speak bitterly of the South African racist system that kept him there, but he did no such thing. Instead, he asked for all South Africans to work together for a better future.

He made this speech shortly after his release from prison in February 1990:

> Today the majority of South Africans, black and white, recognise that **apartheid** has no future. It has to be ended by our own decisive mass action in order to build peace and security.
>
> We have waited too long for our freedom. We can no longer wait.
>
> We call on our white compatriots to join us in the shaping of a new South Africa. The freedom movement is a political home for you too.

'**Apartheid**' in South Africa was a system to keep people separate because of their race.

3. TO CHANGE THE WORLD

Stand against war

American, Helen Keller, was the first deaf–blind person to get a degree from university. She wrote books, spoke for women's rights and argued very strongly against war.

In 1916, World War One was raging in Europe, and Keller made this speech to the Women's Peace Party:

> Strike against war, for without you no battles can be fought.
>
> Strike against manufacturing shrapnel and gas bombs and all other tools of murder.
>
> Strike against preparedness that means death and misery to millions of human beings.
>
> Be not dumb, obedient slaves in an army of destruction. Be heroes in an army of construction.

The space race

In 1961, the Soviets sent the first man into space. American President, John F. Kennedy, wanted to go one better, so he promised the American people that America would be the first country to send a man to the Moon.

Kennedy got his wish in 1969 when American astronaut, Neil Armstrong, was the first man to walk on the Moon.

President Kennedy's speech at Rice University included these words:

> But why, some say, the moon? Why choose this as our goal?
>
> We choose to go to the moon in this decade and do other things, not because they are easy, but because they are hard, because that goal will serve to organize and measure the best of our energies and skills, because that challenge is one that we are willing to accept.

Sadly, Kennedy never got to see the moon landing. He was shot dead in November 1963.

I have a dream

In August 1963, 250,000 people marched on Washington DC, demanding jobs and freedom for all American citizens – black and white.

Martin Luther King was a Church Minister who was going to give a speech at the rally. He had a prepared speech, but then he threw away his notes and said:

> **"** I have a dream that one day this nation will rise up and live out the true meaning of its **creed**: 'We hold these truths to be self-evident: that all men are created equal.'
>
> I have a dream that my four children will one day live in a nation where they will not be judged by the color of their skin but by the content of their character. **"**

When Martin Luther King says '**creed**' he means he is using words from the American Declaration of Independence.

The world-changing teenager

In 2012, Pakistani teenager, Malala Yousafzai, was shot in the head by a member of the militant Taliban group. They shot her because she had written a blog about how hard life was for women under Taliban rule.

But Malala did not die, and when she was well again, she started speaking out against the terrorists and in favour of girls' right to education.

In 2013, Malala made this speech to the United Nations in New York:

> The terrorists thought that they would change my aims and stop my ambitions but nothing changed in my life, except this: weakness, fear and hopelessness died. Strength, power and courage were born.
>
> Let us pick up our books and pens. They are our most powerful weapons. One child, one teacher, one pen and one book can change the world. Education is the only solution. Education first.

In 2014, Malala won the Nobel Peace Prize for her work promoting children's right to education, whoever they are.

4. THE PRESIDENT'S SPEECH

A world at war

In May 1940, France was invaded by the German army. Marshal Philippe Pétain was in charge in France and he was quite happy to see the Germans in control.

Marshal Philippe Pétain

But not all French people agreed. A general in the French army called Charles de Gaulle came to England. He gave a speech on the BBC calling on the French to resist the German invasion:

> I call upon the leaders, together with all soldiers, sailors, and airmen of the French land, sea, and air forces, wherever they may now be, to get in touch with me.
>
> I call upon all Frenchmen who want to remain free to listen to my voice and follow me. Long live free France in honour and independence!

At the end of World War Two, de Gaulle returned to France a hero, and became President of France.

Charles de Gaulle

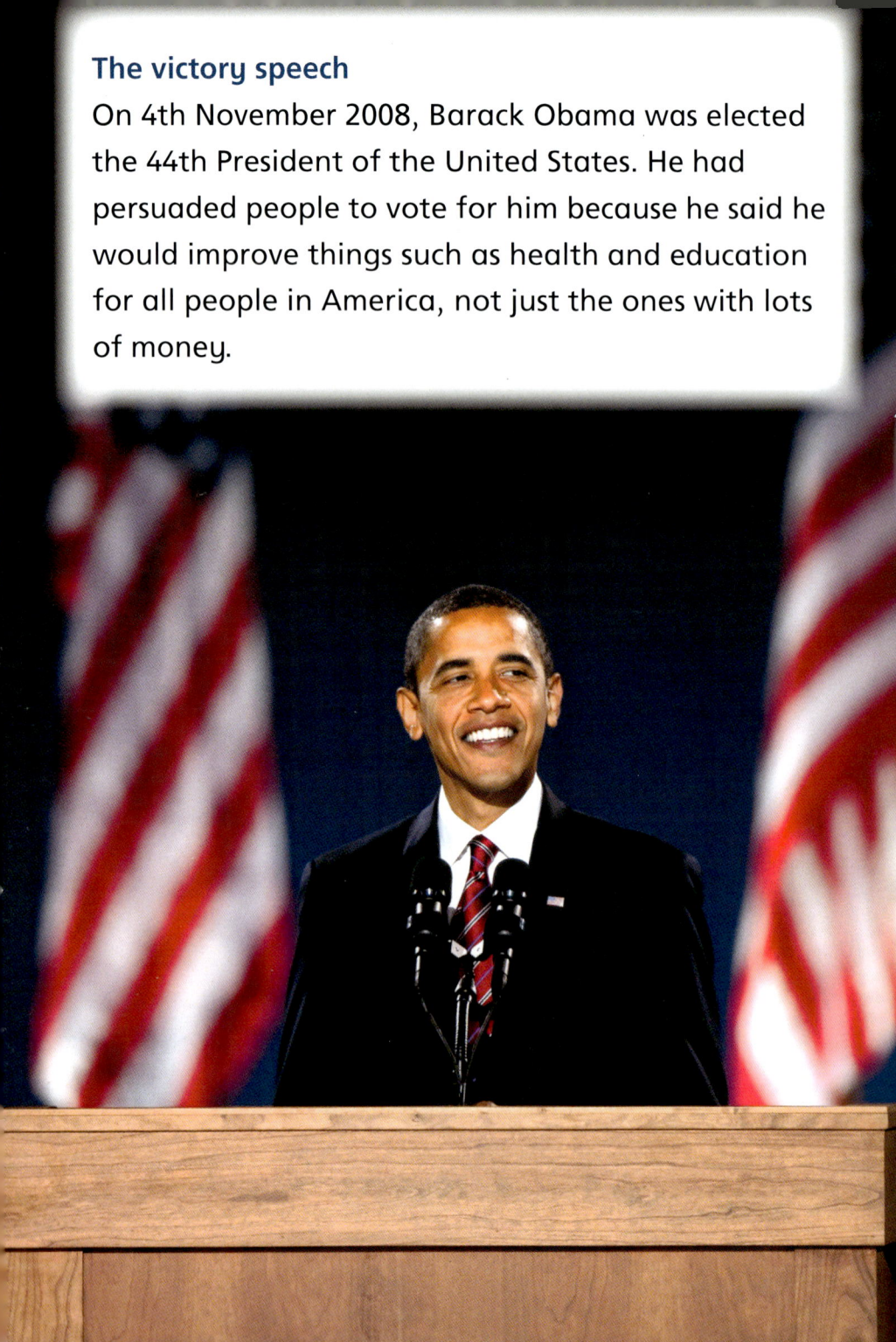

The victory speech

On 4th November 2008, Barack Obama was elected the 44th President of the United States. He had persuaded people to vote for him because he said he would improve things such as health and education for all people in America, not just the ones with lots of money.

He gave this speech in Grant Park, Illinois, watched by hundreds of thousands of people:

> Young and old, rich and poor, Democrat and Republican, black, white, Latino, Asian, Native American, gay, straight, disabled and not disabled – Americans who sent a message to the world that we have never been a collection of Red States and Blue States: we are, and always will be, the United States of America.

Barack Obama was the first ever African American President of the United States.

5. FAMOUS FACES

Famous celebrities have the power to change things with their words, as their fans will listen to them.

Emma Watson's change of role

Emma Watson is best known for her role as Hermione Granger in the Harry Potter films. But in 2014, she gave an important speech to the United Nations.

She spoke about a campaign called HeForShe. The idea of the campaign was to get men to do more to promote equal rights between men and women.

She said:

> **Both men and women should feel free to be sensitive. Both men and women should feel free to be strong.**
>
> **If we stop defining each other by what we are not, and start defining ourselves by who we are, we can all be freer, and this is what HeForShe is about. It's about freedom.**

She is saying that we shouldn't worry about whether we are 'manly' or 'womanly', because we all have different personalities. We should just be ourselves and accept that everybody is equal.

The British Director, Steve McQueen, won an Oscar for his film *12 Years a Slave* at the Academy Awards in 2014.

During his speech, he said his award was for people still in slavery today, such as people who are trafficked and made to work against their will:

" Everyone deserves not just to survive, but to live… …I dedicate this award to all the people who have endured slavery, and the 21 million people who still suffer slavery today. "

Questions

Who was William Wilberforce talking to when he made his anti-slavery speech? (*page 9*)

Why do you think Churchill's 'On the beaches' speech was so powerful? (*pages 12-13*)

What does 'apartheid' mean? (*page 15*)

Did President Kennedy see the moon landing? (*page 19*)

How many people marched on Washington DC demanding jobs and freedom for all Americans? (*Page 20*)

What is special about Barack Obama? (*page 27*)

INDEX

Anthony, Susan B. 10-11
apartheid 15, 31
Armstrong, Neil 18
Churchill, Winston 7, 13
de Gaulle, Charles 25
HeForShe 28-29
Keller, Helen 16-17
Kennedy, John F. 18-19
King, Martin Luther 21
Mandela, Nelson 6, 14
McQueen, Steve 30
Moon (landing) 18-19
Nobel Peace Prize 23
Obama, Barack 26-27, 31
Pétain, Philippe 24
slavery 8, 30
Watson, Emma 28
Wilberforce, William 8-9
World War One 17
World War Two 7, 25
Yousafzai, Malala 7, 22-23